PEACE BE WITH YOU

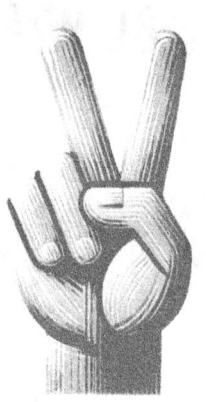

PEACE BE WITH YOU

POEMS, STORIES, & BLURBS

SAM MOODY

7D PRESS

INDIANPOLIS

First Edition

Cover art and illustrations by Sam Moody

This book is dedicated to:

Mom and Dad
Anna
Charlotte and Olivia

CONTENTS

BLURBS

INTRODUCTION

Two years ago, I challenged myself to a little organization project: gather all the things I had written over the past twenty years into one neat-and-tidy package.

I thought it might take a few months. As of today, the job still isn't finished.

As the project took shape, I asked myself two questions: *What types of writing have I enjoyed the most over the years?* And *what, if anything, should I share with the world?*

This book is my answer to those questions.

The bulk of my writing falls into three main categories—**poems**, **stories**, and **blurbs**. Those are now the three sections of this book.

Before you begin reading, here's a short preview of what to expect in each section.

We begin with the **"Poems"** section—my personal favorite. Writing poems helps me wrestle with big ideas, appreciate the gifts I've been given, and slow down to notice the beauty of this simple and complicated life of ours. Think of each poem like a finely cut gemstone. Some will sparkle more than others, depending on the angle you view them from. If you're not sure what to make of one of the poems, check out the reflection questions at the end of the book. Reading poetry isn't for everybody, but hopefully the questions in the back of the book can help you take away something meaningful.

Together, the 14 poems are loosely ordered to mirror life. They move from young to old, innocent to mature, and from birth to death. Or something like that . . .

Next, you'll find the **"Stories"** section. I was once told to judge a short story on three criteria:

Pull—how the story captures and keeps your attention

Clarity of Transport—how clearly your mind is carried into the world of the story

Linger—does the story linger in your mind for one reason or another after putting it down?

When those three things hit, something magical happens. My hope is that someone out there who doesn't love short stories gets to feel that magic while reading this book. And if you *do* love short stories, these are a gift to you from one story lover to another. *Enjoy!*

The **"Blurbs"** section is a bit less straightforward.

I shared an early copy of this book with my friend Jon who, after reading, asked me, *"What exactly constitutes a blurb?"*

Excellent question!

Each blurb is an idea *expanded*.

They all began as a line from a journal entry, a note on my phone, or a comment scribbled in the margin of something I read.

After the fact, I zoomed in, picked the idea apart, and put it back together in a way that's (hopefully) clear, interesting, and easy-to-digest.

These 24 blurbs cover lots of ground, so I'd imagine some will connect with you more than others. Hopefully, at least a few will spark something good in your world.

In all, I'm proud of what this collection represents. It represents that I'm doing the things I teach my students to do—to set meaningful, achievable goals and put in the consistent effort to make them happen. It represents being able to conquer the messiness of my mind and put together something that reflects the values I hold most dear: faith, family, friendship, kindness, creativity, beauty, and joy.

There's a story in here called "**Jamie's Garden**" (p. 37) about a young man who toils for years growing a garden on a piece of land most in town had given up on. After years of steady progress, a magnificent garden finally blooms to life. When the skeptical townsfolk come to see for themselves, Jamie notices an older woman in the crowd—one who had encouraged him while others doubted or scoffed. To thank her, he kneels down and trims a yellow rose from his garden. It's a lovely bloom. He extends the flower and says to her, "This rose. I grew it for you, I think."

This book is my yellow rose.

I wrote it for you, I think.

POEMS

LITTLE BIRD

Little bird, little little bird,
you make each day brighter.
Little bird, little little bird,
you have a light inside you.

Little bird, little little bird,
when you step out from this tree,
Little bird, little little bird,
may the big world set you free.

Little bird, little little bird,
in my heart you'll find a home.
Forever, always, near or far,
you'll never be alone.

And remember all these years from now
when it's time to fly away—
You will always *always* be my little bird.

AWAKE

The breath of dawn's gentle breeze
sweeps away dust and decay
left in winter's wake.

The golden touch of morning's brush
spreads her blues of every hue
through rivers, streams, and lakes.

The bursting gleam of early spring
grows an ever-ending green
while all around the sparrows sing—

Awake! Awake! Awake!

LOVE ME WHOLE

There's a part of me that wants to sing
and a part of me that wants to cry.
There's a part of me that wants to live
and a part that wants to die.

When I'm with you the birdsongs call,
the world is bright and fresh and new.
But when you're gone the world is dark,
the birdsongs stop, the colors fade.

So be with me and love me whole.
Be with me and love me whole.
Be with me and love me whole.
Please be with me and love me whole.

PAW PAW'S HAT

Your Paw Paw loved the Fourth of July
more than anyone I've known.

He flew his flag as proud
as any flag has ever flown.

And every time he wore that hat
with faded stars and stripes,

It made me think this world of ours
may just end up all right.

SET SAIL

The truest of lives
is led by the man
who follows the beat of his drum.
The truest of loves
is found with a girl
to sing and dance along.

You've called her aboard
and charted a course
to a land with the bluest of skies.
Now you'll join in the step
of a song and a dance
that will last all the days of your lives.

Set sail with love,
my friends, set sail,
may your course be steady and true.
Set sail with love,
my friends, set sail,
today we dance for you!

CHARLOTTE'S SONG

After years of patient waiting,
    a daughter was born to us.
She came wrapped in a cruel struggle;
    her breath a whisper,
    her spirit a delicate morning fog.
Standing by her side,
    our hearts weighed heavy like the setting sun
    while hundreds sang of love and mourning.
We summoned the strength of mountains,
    the calm of still waters,
    and the Light of Ages.
On the seventh day, a song returned:
    "See the art in me," the chorus called,
    from Charlotte's heart
    through the breath of the Spirit.
Her song brought peace in knowing
    the masterpiece we held.
Blessed be the name of the Lord,
    the one who brings life,
    who paints each day with hope
    and fills our hearts with joy.

GUIDING LIGHT

Within this empty room
where silence claims the night,
I want to feel your touch
and see your guiding light.

An echoing of hope resounds
deep in my heavy heart.
Together we'll defy the dark
and keep from falling 'part.

FOLKS

Look for folks who hold the door
and nary-ever shout.

Look for folks who fill the cups
of those who pass about.

Look for folks who make you feel
like it's okay to pray.

Look for folks who what they do
lines up with what they say.

GLORY BE TO US ALL

Glory be to us all!
Us *cave dwellers*,
Us *muck-ruckers*,
Us *wretched, reeking, scum-suckers*,
Us *slime*,
Us *ooze*,
Us *gobs*,
Us *goo*—
Glory be to us all!

A THOUSAND MINDS

A thousand minds drift behind
these softly tangled eyes.
Curling slow, a thousand threads
unfurl through surly skies.
Clarity is rare, *a flash*,
then back to swirling air,
where visions burn
and seasons turn
through worlds beyond repair.

WAX FOLK

I'm not sure why
all these wax folk keep
melting
molding
smashing
rolling
shaving
shaping
cutting
pulling
themselves
the ways they do.

It must feel
better
somehow.

THE BOY AND THE KING

Once, long ago, lived an envious king
whose dream was to see the world bend at the knee.
With rage in his veins and a thirst for the fight,
he swore every kingdom would kneel to his might.
He and his armies burned town after town,
leaving puddles of death strewn all 'cross the ground.

Then once, amid slaughter, he held up his hand
as his eyes met the gaze of a dying young man.
The boy had just witnessed unspeakable sins—
the flaying and slaying of all of his kin.
His fate was now written, cruel and unfair,
yet through shattered teeth he whispered a prayer:

Please, Lord, forgive this king.
He killed my father, my mother, my sisters, now me.
But please, Lord, forgive this king.
Show him mercy, dear Father, he couldn't show me.

YOUR DEATH

A crashing wave stole my breath
and slammed me to the ground;
it wracked my chest with heavy sobs
and churned me 'round and 'round.

Then gently with a soothing hand
it laid me to the shore,
shipwrecked, sore, but breathing,
where I cried and cried some more.

Miss you dearly, love you so.
Miss you dearly, love you so.
Miss you dearly, love you so.

I miss you dearly.
I love you so.

PEACE BE WITH YOU

Through the tears of a baby's cry,
Wailing for her mother dear,
Lost in hours and weeks gone by—
Peace be with you.

In the stumbling of a child's first steps,
Scraped knees and fleeting fears,
Seeking comfort in tender arms—
Peace be with you.

In the heart of the teenaged storm,
When nothing seems to make sense,
Yet hopes and dreams begin to form—
Peace be with you.

Setting out upon your own,
As you toss and turn with strength and fear,
Uncovering secrets of life unknown—
Peace be with you.

Juggling love and loss and care,
Daily trials that test your strength,
Through sleepless nights, cruel and unfair—
Peace be with you.

In the twilight of life's turn,
As memories fade and time slows,
Rest thy aching, weary soul—

Peace be with you.
Peace be with you.
Peace be with you.

STORIES

JAMIE'S GARDEN

In the heart of a bustling hillside town lived a young man named Jamie. His bedroom window overlooked the village square where each week farmers came to sell their goods.

Jamie's favorite booth belonged to an old gardener from beyond the countryside who sold bouquets of wildflowers—each a delicate spill of natural blooms. Black-eyed Susans, bluebells, and Queen Anne's lace sat nestled among feathery greens. Asters, goldenrod, and wands of prairie sage were clustered in dainty bunches, knotted with strands of silk and twine.

Each Sunday, Jamie bought a bouquet from the old man's cart and placed it on the window ledge overlooking the town square.

One Sunday, however, the old gardener's booth sat empty. Asking around, Jamie discovered the gardener had become ill and his land was to be sold off for harvest. Jamie's heart broke. The flowers had brought him such joy through the years. He decided in that moment he would become a gardener and bring his own flowers to market one day.

Some time had passed when it came to Jamie's attention that a plot of land just outside town was up for sale at a reasonable cost. The land was being sold for almost nothing, yet nobody in town wanted anything to do with it.

Jamie asked around about the land, but all who knew it were skeptical.

"That piece of land is wild and unruly."

"It's not worth the trouble."

"A worthless lot. I'd stay far away."

Struck with a curious spirit, Jamie ventured out to explore this so-called 'worthless' piece of land with his own eyes. He had heard the land was barren—a complete waste of time and money—but as he walked the grounds he recognized many of the blooms from the old man's booth. Purple coneflowers sprang up like tiny bonfires amidst the tangled grasses while shy forget-me-nots peeked their blue-petaled heads out from the overgrowth. Golden buttercups dotted the landscape like scattered coins ready to be collected.

With a hopeful heart and a small cash offer, Jamie bought the land and moved from the city. He told anyone who asked that he planned to turn his new land into a beautiful garden.

They scoffed.

Still, a few curious townsfolk ventured out to see Jamie's garden for themselves. To their amusement, it was just as overgrown as they had remembered. One man, shaking his head, saw Jamie and shouted, "You'll never grow anything worthwhile here. You're wasting your time!"

Jamie heard the words, but unlike the townsfolk, he felt life in this place. Yes, it was overgrown, but the wildflowers grew strong. He knew he could turn this land into something wonderful. He put his head down, grabbed a shovel, and went to work.

As the townsfolk dispersed, one woman lingered, her expression softer than the others. She didn't speak. She simply watched Jamie as he surveyed the land, a faint curiosity in her eye.

Days turned to weeks and Jamie's dedication only grew stronger. He whittled away at the overgrowth, then tilled the soil inch by inch. He danced when it rained and sang with the whistling wind. His garden was growing, slowly but steadily, under his loving watch.

Seasons came and went, and every so often the curious townsfolk wandered by. Old neighbors would sometimes wave Jamie over and try to talk some sense into him.

"Jamie—all these years you've spent toiling under the sun. And for what? It's not quite coming along yet is it?"

Jamie thanked his old neighbors for their visits, but assured them there was more work to be done. He nodded his head, grabbed his trusty shovel, and went back about his business.

From time to time, the same lingering woman would pass by Jamie's plot. Her visits became something like a quiet ritual. While others mocked or questioned, she would simply pause at the edge of the field, her gaze steadily fixed on Jamie's progress.

Once, on one particularly gray afternoon, the woman walked along the edge of the garden. This time, she stepped closer, bending down to examine a patch of newly planted seedlings.

"These will do well here," she said, almost to herself.

It was the gentlest of acknowledgements, but it warmed Jamie's heart all the same.

Years passed and Jamie worked day-in and day-out to bring his garden to life. Most of the townsfolk had stopped visiting, but the older woman continued stopping by from time to time.

At the end of a long, hard winter, frost lifted its frozen spell from the land and gave way to the warmth of early spring.

Jamie's garden began to bloom.

He walked the grounds each morning, speaking to each young sprig. His fingers and palms were dark with soil, but his spirit glowed golden bright. Jamie had poured himself into the earth beneath him, and the soil was now bringing new life.

Later that season, a group of curious townsfolk returned once again. Their once-doubting hearts were struck with silent awe. Jamie's garden was in full bloom.

Crimsons rich as pomegranates, blues soft as robins' eggs, violets so deep they seemed to drink in the midday sun. Rosebuds twirled around trellises, foxgloves and hollyhocks swayed their dew-spotted bells to-and-fro. Sweet dahlias with petals like painted fire, lilies dressed in speckled orange-cream dresses, the silken blush of peony bouquets. Honeysuckle twined along the garden's gate, greeting visitors with its sweet perfume.

"Is this the same place?" they gasped. "It can't be."

Jamie's heart swelled with pride and he noticed the old woman smiling at the edge of the crowd.

Kneeling down, he found the most exquisite yellow rose one could imagine. He gently trimmed the velvet bloom from its bush and brought it to the woman who had become something like a friend.

"This rose," Jamie said. "I grew it for you, I think."

Her eyes softened, filling with a memory that seemed to come alive as she gazed at the flower.

"It reminds me of the wildflowers my husband used to sell," she said.

A single tear traced its way down her cheek, catching the sun like a drop of morning rain.

BENNY'S FIRST FORAGE

Golden morning sunbeams kiss awake the big wide world. Benny ruffles his feathers, excited for a new day of summer adventure.

"Mom, Dad—I'm hungry!" Benny chirps, morning light glittering in his eyes.

Mom and Dad exchange a knowing glance.

"Benny, how would you like to forage your own meal today?" Mom asks with a grin.

"Forage my own meal?" Benny's feathers quiver with excitement. "Yes, yes! Please, yes!"

"Okay son, follow me," Benny's dad says as he leaps out of the nest into a draft of springtime breeze. They soar far above the green meadows below.

"Your first lesson is to follow your nose."

Follow my nose, Benny thinks.

He breathes in deeply and his senses come alive—fresh cut grass, cherry blossom nectar, the scent of a rabbit down below . . . then—*ta-da!*—a berry bush appears!

The family swoops down as Benny pops a plump berry into his beak.

"These berries taste like sugar and sunshine," Benny says as the family enjoys their blackberry feast.

As they prepare to leave, a dark shadow passes overhead. Benny's heart beats against his chest.

"It's a crow," Mom whispers, her eyes narrowing.

The crow caws a warning from above:

"My territory!" it squawks. "My territory!"

Benny looks up and sees the crow's piercing black eyes.

"Don't worry, Benny. Just stay close," Dad says, his voice steady and alert.

Suddenly, the wind picks up. *Sha-whoosh!* The leaves rustle like a thousand tambourines, unsettling the crow.

"Now's our chance!" Mom signals, and they dart away, leaving the cawing crow far behind.

Back home in the nest, Benny and his family snuggle tight. The sky turns dark orange as the setting sun dips against the horizon.

"I was scared today," Benny says.

"Yes, but you were also brave," Mom says. "I'm proud of you."

"What a day," Dad coos softly as the world begins its evening lullaby.

As nighttime falls, a web of twinkling stars dances alongside the fireflies, glittering their magic spells across the sleepy prairie.

"Goodnight," Benny whispers, closing his eyes, his heart as full as his body is tired.

"Goodnight Benny," Mom and Dad whisper as the big wide world falls fast asleep.

SORRY, HONEY

Nestled in a modern suburb known for technology and comfort, the Redmon family home is the paragon of new-age convenience.

Edwin Redmon, a young designer and technological visionary, works dozens of projects at once thanks to his new virtual chamber. He had it installed last fall in his home office.

Edwin's wife Eliza also runs a thriving online empire selling glamorous electronic accessories. Her brand, Cosmè, is scheduled to debut a new ad next month in *Vanity*.

The Redmons' life pulses with passion and energy.

Their young daughter Lenore is cut from the same cloth. Her insatiable curiosity and unstoppable drive helps her excel in her schoolwork while receiving top marks for both character and academic potential. Her parents are convinced their daughter will one day run her own company, if not the entire planet. She is everything they had hoped for in a child. They could not be more proud.

One early summer evening, with sunbeams streaming through slitted shades, young Lenore places the final touches on her latest artistic masterpiece—a pencil sketch of her family swimming in the neighbor's new swimming pool. Her parents had promised they would take her swimming for the first time this week. Her chest swells with excitement as she holds her drawing up to the light. It feels like a ticket to the magical day she's been waiting for.

Lenore runs down the stairs and flits across the living room toward her parents' offices. "Daddy, Mommy, look at my picture," Lenore says. "I drew us all swimming at the Johnsons' new pool."

"Just a second, Lenore," Edwin murmurs, his gaze fixed on the swirling designs unfolding across holographic screens.

"Can it wait a few minutes, sweetie?" Eliza adds, fingers dancing over her tablet keys.

Lenore's smile falters. She lowers the drawing slightly and glances between her parents, but they don't look up. Her heels sink down into the plush carpet fibers and she turns back toward her room, drawing in hand.

"Sorry, honey!" her mom calls from behind.

At her bedroom desk once again, Lenore looks down at her drawing. It really is quite the scene. Every detail is just right. The ripples on the water, the branches on the tree, her parents and her splashing together in the water.

Next comes the color.

Carefully selecting four shades, she blends together a sparkling blue across the pool's surface. Next she adds pink and purple flowers lining the poolside. Then red and orange for the brick pillars, black and gray for the gate and three shades of green for the bushes and trees.

It's lovely.

Her room is quiet. The hum of the house is steady but distant, her parents' voices muffled behind closed office doors.

Sweet Lenore snuggles up under her bedsheets, closes her eyes, and is soon dreaming of backstrokes and swan dives across crystalline pools stretched between towering cloud-castles.

* * *

The next morning, sunlight floods through linen curtains casting a warm glow across Lenore's bedroom.

Edwin hurries down the hall, preparing for another busy day.

The morning routine gets off and running as Lenore sees her gown for the day, pressed and ready, hanging on a knob of the dresser.

Her eyes fall on the drawing she made the night before and her heart jumps. *Today could be the day*, she thinks.

At the breakfast table, Lenore waits for a moment where her dad is not checking his messages. He puts his tablet down and sighs, poking at the last few bits of omelet on his plate.

This is her moment.

"Daddy?"

"Yes, honey?"

"Could we do a swim lesson today?"

His eyebrows pinch together above his nose. He takes a slow, deep breath through his nose.

"Maybe tomorrow," he says. "I have a project to finish. Sorry, honey."

Lenore stares down at the last few marshmallows floating on the surface of her cereal bowl. She doesn't answer.

* * *

Evening comes. With her parents absorbed in work, Lenore sits again at her desk, staring longingly at her colorful drawing. She has an idea.

Taking her pencil in hand, she turns the eraser toward the page and begins rubbing away at the outline of her mom and dad. When she's done brushing away the pink dust it's just her in the pool—a little girl swimming alone.

With a grin, she slides open a dresser drawer and slips on the bathing suit she picked out last week. It's a purple one-piece with ruffles on the shoulders.

Pulling open her closet door, she grabs a bath towel and throws it over her shoulder.

The hallway is dark except for the faint glow of her parents' offices. She pauses, clutching the towel, listening for voices or footsteps. Nothing. Just the soft whirring of electronic machines.

Lenore skirts past her father's office, breath caught in her throat. She hesitates for a moment. What would her parents do if they caught her? The thought flutters through her mind.

Sliding out the side door, Lenore steps into the warm night air. She tucks her towel under her arm and slips across the yard.

The moon hangs rare and radiant above her.

She lifts the gate's latch and clicks it gently back in place behind her.

Silent and barefoot, Lenore waltzes toward the water.

Stifling a giggle, Lenore touches her heels against the water's surface, sending reflected moonbeams fluttering across the pool. The stillness of night fills the open sky.

She pauses for a moment and looks back toward her house. The glow of her parents' offices shines out into the night. Would they notice if she were gone?

Dangling her legs in the water, she imagines her toes are orange and webbed like a duck's. Warm water tickles the skin between them. She hadn't expected the pool to be so toasty. It's perfect.

Holding fast to the steel gutter, Lenore slides her body into the water. The waterline climbs up her swimsuit. It feels like stepping into an endless bathtub. Her breath catches in her chest as her nerves begin to flutter.

Crisp and clear, the depths glow purple-blue, disappearing to an empty black below. "How deep is a swimming pool?" she wonders.

For the first time, the silence feels heavy. The stillness of the water holds its breath around her.

Anxious to swim, Lenore bobs up and down—up and down—even dunking her whole head underwater, just like she does in the bath. Her feet plunge downward but find only the empty dark below. After a few seconds, she pulls herself back to the surface.

She swings her legs up longways across the pool's edge. To her delight, her legs float like innertubes, bobbing her knees and toes above the surface.

She giggles louder now and hears herself echo across the silent yard.

Closing her eyes, Lenore breathes deep to calm herself down. Her parents would be very upset if they found her swimming in the neighbors' pool by herself.

With the deep breath inside her lungs, her chest fills and her body begins floating to the edge of the mirrored surface, holding her up like a lily pad.

She smiles beneath the black sky.

Tonight is a dream come true.

As she breathes out, her chest dips below the waterline. A quick exhale and the water feels heavier. She reaches for the edge of the pool, but it's no longer there. Her heart thumps against her ribs as the dark water pulls at her legs.

* * *

Inside the house, Edwin passes by his daughter Lenore's room and notices her clothes strewn across the floor. He smiles at the colorful drawing on her desk admiring the gently blended hues.

The window is cracked. Outside, he hears the faint sound of someone splashing in the pool next door.

The soft buzz of his wristband catches his attention—a call from tomorrow morning's client. With a flick of his thumb, he answers and heads back to his office, ready for a long night.

54

ROBBIE THE ROBOT

Gears whirr and lights flicker to life as dawn breaks over Robot City. Robbie the Robot zips out of bed, eager for another busy robot day. As he stretches his sprockets, his circuits spark and he notices something new—a freshly installed dial on his chest labeled "Kindness."

"I wonder what this does?" Robbie says to himself.

Without a second thought, he cranks the knob up all the way. He feels his chipset warm and his eyes glow a bit brighter.

"Ooh, that feels nice," he says, ready to head out into the bustling streets of Robot City.

His first stop is at the city park where the sound of birds chirping and machinery humming fills the air. As Robbie zooms around, he notices a small robot struggling to plant a tree. The little robot's arms aren't long enough to dig the hole, and it spins its gears in frustration. Robbie, his kindness dial turned all the way up, zips over in a flash.

"Let me help!" he offers, using his long arms to dig a perfect hole.

When Robbie finishes planting the tree, the little robot buzzes a happy, "Thank you!"

Robbie's circuits sing with joy, warming him all the way down to his circuitboard.

After leaving the park, Robbie makes his way to Factory Square where robots of all sizes move pieces of machinery with clockwork precision. As he crosses the square, Robbie spots a larger robot whose rusted arms are stuck beneath the weight of a heavy load. Without hesitation Robbie rushes to its aid.

"Don't worry, I've got this!" he says as he whips out his emergency toolkit.

His arms fly around tightening bolts, greasing gears, and oiling sprockets until the large robot's arms move freely once again.

"Thank you, young man," the rusty robot says, waving its newly repaired arms in appreciation. Robbie smiles and gives the robot a hearty embrace, his kindness still flowing at full throttle.

Robbie makes his way down Electron Avenue, a busy street lined with neon signs for shops and vendors. Along the side of the road he spots a group of young schoolbots huddled together looking for an opening to cross. The traffic on Electron Avenue is relentless. Robbie doesn't hesitate. He darts out into the street, waving his arms to stop the oncoming cars.

"Go ahead, you can cross now!" he calls to the schoolbots, who scurry across to safety. Their little voices chirp in gratitude, and Robbie's heart circuits swell once again. The cars in the street honk their horns, swerving around Robbie as he darts back to the sidewalk and goes along his way.

All day long Robbie whirrs from place to place doing everything he can for his fellow neighbor bots. He hauls a load of old spark plugs, pushes a broken down trike bot, and even gives a few jolts of charge to an elderly bot down on her luck.

As the sun sets over Robot City, Robbie's energy is near zero. His battery, glowing so strong that morning, now blinks a weary red. Rolling toward his bed, Robbie collapses into an exhausted heap and is snoring within seconds.

. . . flurr-thump . . . flurr-thump . . . flurr-thump . . .

* * *

The next morning, Robbie wakes up creaky and sore. His circuits sputter a bit and he has to pop a gear back in place that came loose overnight.

"Whew . . . I think overdid it yesterday," he says to himself.

Remembering the new dial on his chest, Robbie decides to turn it all the way down to zero.

He feels the whirring in his chest slow down, then come to a complete stop. A cold mechanical metronome begins clicking to a steady beat.

"That should do the trick," he says. "Let's get going. So much to do today."

As he zips through the city park once again, Robbie sees the same small robot from yesterday struggling to plant another tree. This time, instead of helping, Robbie zooms right past without a second glance.

"Not today," he grumbles, ignoring the little bot's call for help. Robbie's metronome clicks with indifference as he makes his way through the crowd toward Factory Square.

At Factory Square, the scene is familiar. The same rusted robot is once again stuck, its arms grinding under the weight of heavy crates. Robbie sees it, but instead of rushing to help, he keeps rolling along unbothered.

"Fix it yourself," he mumbles, focusing on his own agenda. The rusted robot looks after him helplessly, its arm hopelessly jammed.

As Robbie speeds down Robot Avenue, a gaggle of anxious schoolbots once again waits at the crosswalk, but this time Robbie doesn't even slow down. His metronome tells him there's no time to help the schoolbots. "They need to learn how to cross the street themselves," he says to himself as he zips across the street to his next appointment.

For the rest of the day Robbie ticks along, checking item after item off his list. He never once stops to talk to his neighbor bots.

By nightfall, Robbie's battery still has quite a bit of charge, but his chest circuits feel cold and empty. He tries to power down, but a nagging feeling inside keeps him awake.

"I've never felt this way before," he thinks to himself. Then he realizes what that feeling is coming from. His internal screen is showing a reel of all the times he decided not to help his neighbor bots. Robbie gives a heavy sigh, thinking about how cold he had been to the bots in his neighborhood. He sinks into his bed, wondering what he could have done differently.

Before dozing off, Robbie remembers the kindness dial. He reaches down and eases the knob up to a comfortable level—high enough that it feels warm, but not so intense that he can't fall asleep.

"It's okay, Robbie. You'll do better tomorrow," he says to himself while drifting off to sleep.

* * *

Robbie wakes up the next morning eager to start the day. The extremes of the past two days are still fresh in his mind, and he already feels that today will be better.

With his kindness dial turned to a comfy-and-warm but not-too-overwhelming level, he sets out once again into a bustling day of robot life.

At the park, Robbie sees the small robot, still working diligently on its trees. This time, Robbie stops to help for a few minutes. He helps dig a small hole and offers some tips for planting the tree. Then he steps back and lets the young bot keep at it.

"Looks like you have it from here!" he says kindly, watching as the little bot attacks the job with newfound confidence. Robbie smiles and heads down the road toward Factory Square.

At Factory Square, who does Robbie encounter but the rusty older robot who keeps getting his arms stuck. Robbie offers just enough help to loosen the stuck arm and shows the robot how to oil its own gears.

"Keep those rusty gears greased, my friend! If you don't, you'll keep getting your arms stuck." The robot gives a grateful nod and gets back to work.

When Robbie reaches Robot Avenue, he sees the schoolbots waiting once again. This time, instead of halting traffic for them, he rolls over, gets their attention, and teaches the whole group how to read the crossing signal.

"Now you can cross safely on your own!" he says, watching proudly as they use the signal to navigate the crosswalk all by themselves.

Robbie goes about his day, finding ways to help, but also taking good care of the things he needs to do. He replaces a few springs in his roller-gears and enjoys a stroll along the boardwalk on the edge of town.

As evening falls, Robbie returns home, his battery humming contentedly. His energy is low, but his chest feels warm and full. His heart circuits glows a gentle, peaceful blue.

"Today was a very good day," he says to himself.

It was a very good day, indeed.

Robbie's internal screen flashes with memories of his neighbor bots and the difference he made for them.

The glow of memories begins to fade as his circuits slow down and Robbie falls into a deep and peaceful sleep.

A BARGAIN

In a world balanced precariously between the tangible and the fantastical, The Visionary is an enigma wrapped in mystery. His mansion, eclipsed by rumors and myths, looms on the outskirts of a town forgotten by progress and time.

A heavy knock echoes as weighted iron thunks against weathered wood. The Visionary approaches the door eager to see who fate has brought today. He ushers his visitor in with a dramatic gesture worthy of a stage.

"Welcome, welcome! Come in, come in!"

Before him stands a tired woman. Her eyes are dark with desperation, and her voice wavers as she speaks. "I've reached the end of my rope. My well has run dry. I need something . . . a spark . . . anything . . . I've heard you can help me."

"Intriguing," The Visionary says, a grin stretching across his veiled face. "I believe you've come to the right place. Follow me."

A door creaks open revealing a dimly lit corridor.

As they float through labyrinthine halls, the air pulses with whispers of half-dreams. The sound of their breath presses against the walls as time itself bends around them.

After some combination of seconds and years, they reach the core of The Visionary's realm.

"This, I believe, is what you've come for."

A final doorway opens to reveal an impossible light. They stand together in a place that feels both everywhere and nowhere.

The woman's eyes fall upon a glowing orb in the center of the room.

"What . . . is it?" asks the woman.

"Touch it," says The Visionary.

The woman moves closer. Her eyes widen. She reaches a finger out to touch the light. An infinite warmth fills every fiber of her being. A flash of swirling color appears as light breaks into a million crystal shards of time and space. The artist's dreams flicker around the room, each one deeper and more breathtaking than the last.

She feels a hand on her shoulder, and the infinite dreamworld falls away in a cloud of smoky dust. She catches her breath, eyes wide, still entranced by the glowing energy that had radiated around them.

"Are you interested?"

"Yes. I'm interested," she says quickly, failing to hide her desperation. "But what does it cost?"

"A fair price."

"I don't have much money."

"It won't cost you any money at all."

The Visionary smiles, eyes twinkling.

"Think of it like a bargain."

"I'm not sure I understand," the woman says.

"I give you something you want; you give me something I want. That's the bargain."

"Well, what do you want? I've told you already, I have no money. I hardly own a thing."

The Visionary's heavy gaze presses against the woman. He lets her grow increasingly uncomfortable before breaking the silence.

"I propose a trade," he says. "You use my machine as much as you please—*forever*. All I ask in return is a small piece of your . . . *self.*"

The woman thinks quickly. A part of her *self*? Her *hair*? Her *eyes*? Her *arms*? Her *legs*? What could she part with? What would he want? What did he mean?

"Well, what exactly did you have in mind? I could give you my hair. I could certainly do without my hair."

The Visionary laughs. "No, no no, my dear. I have no need for your hair. Or your eyes. Or your arms or legs."

She shuddered.

"No, sweet darling, I don't desire your body—I need a piece of your *self*. Your *being* . . . I'm not sure quite how else to put it."

The woman's eyes narrow, perplexed at the Visionary's words.

The Visionary reaches a long hand out toward her heart, gesturing to touch the side of her head.

"May I?"

She nods.

As his cold hand presses just below her temple, she feels a stirring beneath the surface of her mind. Her awareness drops like an anchor into a deep chamber locked far away inside a realm she had never explored.

She feels his hand reach out and lift something small and delicate.

A wooden box.

He opens it.

They look inside.

She smiles.

Inside is a small but brilliant light. A thousand weightless constellations, shifting and shaping in a glimmering dance.

Yes. She knows this light well. It has been with her from the very beginning. It has always been there.

A teardrop slips down her cheek as she thinks about letting it go.

Time slows. Hours—*years, perhaps*—go by before she looks back to the Visionary. He stands unmoved.

"A bargain?"

The Visionary's lips do not move; his voice is buried deep in the caverns of her mind.

A bargain.

She agrees.

An impossible light flickers. She shuts her eyes. In a moment she opens them to find a blank canvas staring back where the Visionary had just stood. She is in her studio, alone and weary, yet her hands seem to know exactly what to do.

She paints furiously, day and night. Her creations transcend realms of the known, reaching into the space between Heaven and Earth—between life and death. Colors blend in ways no eyes could even dream. Each brushstroke is its own dream. Her work is magnificent, each piece more profound than the last.

Packed shows soon follow, walls lined with her canvases, the air buzzing with whispers of admiration. Bidding wars break out, and the newspapers heap glowing praise on her exhibitions. The life she once dreamed of—wealth, fame, recognition—is now her own. She is the artist *en vogue*, her name uttered in reverence.

But as each masterpiece materializes, a void begins hollowing her from the inside out. The more her hands create, the more she feels something slipping away. Nights grow long, her sleep grows restless. This gnawing emptiness; this dull aching dread. It grows right in the place where those constellations used to be. Darkness seeps out, swallowing up all the light in its path.

With each applause and accolade, the void grows deeper, stronger, heavier.

She pushes herself harder, painting more frantically, hoping that the next piece will bring back what she has lost. But the abyss expands, swallowing every fleck of joy. The colors, once vibrant in her mind, are now dull. The energy that flowed so freely is now a pale echo of what once was.

Hollow, and more empty than before, she returns to The Visionary's mansion, pushing her way through doorways and rooms, searching for him.

"Help me! Please! Help me!" she cries.

The Visionary appears. He watches her for a moment with detached curiosity, head tilted slightly.

"Help you?"

His voice hangs in the stillness.

"My dear—haven't I done just that? Your work is magnificent. I've read your reviews in the papers. Truly remarkable."

She shakes her head, hands clenched into white-knuckled fists. She glares at The Visionary. "It's not me!" She screams. "None of it! I can't live this way. I need it back. Give it back, please!"

She takes a shuddering breath.

The Visionary's lips curve in a slow smile. He regards her for a long moment.

"I'm afraid that's not the way this works, child," The Visionary replies.

Their eyes meet, and for a fleeting second, she glimpses something familiar—a far-off galaxy, flickering with sparks and flames, spinning at the outer edges of a distant universe.

Then it all turns to dust.

Her eyes open to a blank canvas staring back at her.

She wipes a single tear from her cheek.

And she paints the darkness.

For the darkness is all she knows.

THE BALLAD OF WILLARD MCFEE

A long time ago in the Yimmerlyn Sea,
in a sandy sea cave lived Willard McFee.

Most days old Willard would scrunch up in a hunch,
for Willard McFee wasn't happy a bunch.

Deep in the sea he moaned and he groaned
about how he would be there forever alone.

So how did this woeful tale begin?
Let's go back and tell it from beginning to end.

Willard was joyful, his spirit was free,
a beloved young man was Willard McFee.

His wife was Elmira Tamira Sheroo
who he met on a walk through the Yimmerlyn Zoo.

They married in spring under blossoming trees
with petals that danced on a glittering breeze.

Their love was enormous, their life was just grand,
they had every last bit of this life of theirs planned.

But once on a fateful midsummer's eve,
Willard McFee took his boat out to sea.

He told his Elmira Tamira Sheroo,
"I'll be back in a jiffy—an hour or two!"

But that night wasn't right when his boat left for sea
and away from the shore went Willard McFee.

An hour went by, and McFee fell asleep,
he slept as his boat drifted out to the deep.

He awoke to a wave so mighty and wide
that it blocked out the stars and the moon and the sky.

He shouted, *"Oh no! Oh my! Oh me!"*
as the wave knocked Willard McFee to the sea.

Holding his breath and closing his eyes,
the wave took Willard McFee for a ride.

Past fishes much bigger than whales and sharks,
past unicorn fish and prickly larks!

After a while he splished and he sploshed
to a big sandy cave where he finally stopped.

A day turned to seven, then fifty, then more,
and life under-sea was a terrible bore.

Willard would lay with his head in his hands,
hoping to see his Elmira again.

One day he tried swimming, he geared up to go,
but he didn't go far, and he went very slow.

His arms were too tired, his legs were too weak,
so he turned back around and fell back to sleep.

His body and heart were aching and sore,
but that night was the night he'd been waiting for . . .

Deep in his sleep McFee had a dream
about taking a ride to the top of the sea.

In the dream he shrank small and jumped into a bubble,
which floated him up and away from his trouble.

The dream was a dream, but when he awoke,
Willard McFee shouted, *"I'm gonna float!"*

*"Float up in a bubble, float up to the sky,
to be with my love 'til the day that I die!"*

And that marked the day that Willard McFee
started building his giant air bubble machine.

He worked every day at a feverish pace,
but it still took him years to get it in place.

With seaweed and wood and a fish-powered sucker,
he sucked up some air to an air-bubble puffer.

He started the bubble with sea snail goo,
which stayed mighty strong as it grew and it grew.

The bubble got bigger and bigger it got,
then Willard McFee started floating up top.

Past whales and whippets and starfish he flew,
up to Elmira Tamira Sheroo.

He burst through the waves and into the air,
the sun struck his face, the breeze swept his hair.

He swam to the shore which took all his might,
the waves battled strong, but he won the fight.

He ran through the streets that he once called home,
searching and searching, he roamed and he roamed.

Then finally, wonderfully, who should he see?
Elmira Tamira, as fair as could be.

"I thought you were lost to the depths of the sea!"
she cried, as she kissed her dear Willard McFee.

They laughed and they danced 'til the breaking of dawn,
grateful their terrible nightmare was gone.

And sailors who pass through the Yimmerlyn Sea
still sing the Ballad of Willard McFee.

The sailor who floated from deep ocean blue
to return to his love, his Elmira Sheroo.

BLURBS

PART 1

ON LIFE AND LIVING

6 THINGS EVERYONE CAN AND SHOULD DO

Treat others the way you would like to be treated. This rule will help you guide your interactions with others. Remember—the best way to make a friend is to be a friend. Always err on the side of kindness.

Set goals and work toward them. Having clear goals keeps you focused and motivated. Working toward goals gives you a sense of purpose and accomplishment. *Reevaluate your goals regularly!*

Practice gratitude. Taking time to reflect on the things you are thankful for helps you shift your focus to the positive aspects of your life and increases your sense of fulfillment. BONUS POINTS if you make it a habit to *share* your gratitude with others in a meaningful way.

Stay curious and open-minded. Keeping an open mind and a willingness to try new things will help you grow and expand your horizons. *Always ask questions. Always wonder. Always move forward.*

Take care of yourself. Taking care of your physical, mental, and emotional health is foundational to daily life. Prioritize your health and wellbeing by making time for daily activities that nourish and support you and your personal needs. Suggestion—if you can, share some of these activities with family and friends.

Check in on your people. Who are the people in your life that matter most? The people who you rely on? The people who rely on you? Check in on them. Follow up. And don't just think about them—talk to them and intentionally show you care. People matter! Treat them well.

A LESSON IN CHARACTER

People throw around the phrase "strong character" like it's an obvious thing. But what does "strong character" actually mean?

At its core, character is about who you are when no one's watching. It's your moral backbone—your integrity, resilience, courage, honesty, humility, and compassion. A person with strong character consistently does the right thing, even when it's inconvenient. A person with weak character? They bend to whatever's easiest, whatever benefits them in the moment.

The way we see character in people is the same way we see it in books: through actions, words, and choices. In storytelling, characterization is how a writer reveals a character's true nature—through what they say, how they treat others, and the decisions they make under pressure. It works the same way in real life. You don't really know someone until you've seen how they handle adversity, how they respond to failure, how they treat people who can't do anything for them. A person might say they're honest and upstanding, but if they consistently cut corners and cave to temptation when no one's looking, their actions tell a different story.

The good news? Character isn't set in stone. Just like in a novel, people change and grow—sometimes even transform. A selfish person can learn to be selfless. A coward can develop courage. A liar can choose to tell the truth. But change doesn't happen by accident. Change is forged through struggle, self-reflection, and repeated choices.

At the end of the day, character isn't about how you want to be seen; it's about how you actually are. And just like in great stories, what really matters isn't where you started, or where you've been—what matters most is where you go from here.

FLOW: THE HEART OF FOCUS

The concept of flow was originally introduced by Mihaly Csikszentmihaly in his 1990 book, *Flow: The Psychology of Optimal Experience.* Whether you are coding, painting, writing, or solving complex problems, achieving flow is like finding yourself in an intricate dance where each step leads naturally to the next. You're not just involved; you're completely engrossed, using your mental and physical abilities to their fullest, most realized extent.

Imagine you're climbing a rock face. Each hold is a new challenge, and as you climb, there's no room in your mind for distractions. You're not just climbing; you're in a constantly evolving dialogue with the rock—each move an exercise of call-and-response. All of your senses are attuned to the task at hand. The freeing focus silences the noise in your head, and for as long as it lasts, you are the climb.

Finding yourself in a flow state is mesmerizing. Here are eight characteristics of flow that can help you better understand this elusive but captivating state of mind, and can hopefully help you capture it when you need it most.

During flow . . .

Goals Are Clear and Engaging: When you're in flow, your objectives are unmistakable. You're not lost or confused about what you're supposed to do. Each step in your task is clear, much like how each sentence in a gripping book leads you to the next. This clarity keeps you anchored and guides your actions, providing a sense of direction and purpose. The immediate feedback you receive, whether from the task itself or your own recognition of progress, keeps you engaged and on track.

The Challenge Matches Your Skills: In this state, the difficulty of what you're doing is perfectly tuned to your abilities. It's not so easy that you're bored, but not so hard that you're overwhelmed. Think of it like skiing down a slope that pushes you to be at your best. Your senses are fully tuned in to what's coming next. This is not cruise-control; it's an appropriate challenge that brings out the best you have to offer.

Your Actions and Awareness Become One: When deeply in flow, there's a seamless integration of your actions and your awareness. You're not overthinking or analyzing each move; instead, you're moving instinctively, trusting yourself and your abilities. You're not consciously directing each motion; your body just knows what to do. This harmony allows for a smooth and uninterrupted experience. This doesn't mean you aren't thinking—it means your thoughts, actions, and reactions are all firing in real time to achieve a desired outcome.

All Distractions Melt Away: In this state, the regular distractions that might normally pull your attention away seem to vanish. It's just you and the task at hand. The usual cacophony of thoughts, worries, and external stimuli fades into the background, leaving a clear, unobstructed focus on your activity.

Fear of Failure Disappears: In the midst of flow, fear and anxiety about failing don't find a foothold. You're too wrapped up in the task, too committed to the moment. This lack of fear allows for a freer, more creative approach to your work. You're not held back by the concern of making mistakes, which often leads to more innovative and authentic results.

Self-Consciousness Gives Way to Pure Engagement: Building on the previous point, when in a flow state, self-reflection and self-criticism take a back seat. You're not judging yourself, not worrying about how you appear or perform. This absence of self-consciousness frees you to be completely immersed in your activity, allowing for a depth of engagement that is rare and fulfilling.

Time Becomes Elastic and Unimportant: One of the most striking aspects of flow is how it warps your sense of time. Hours can pass in what feels like minutes, or moments can stretch out and gain a depth that seems to hold so much more. A Premier League forward about to strike a free kick takes in an encyclopedia's worth of input before making his strike. Your senses are totally in tune with your body and performance. The altered perception of time is a testament to how engrossing the flow state is.

The Joy of the Activity Is Its Own Reward: In flow, the activity itself is so inherently satisfying that external rewards or recognition become secondary. You're not driven by the desire for accolades or external validation; instead, the sheer joy and fulfillment of doing becomes the primary motivator. This intrinsic motivation is often what leads to the most passionate and heartfelt work.

To conclude, tapping into flow can be transformative. It's not just about productivity or creativity; it's about connecting deeply with the moment. Finding flow can be elusive—it requires the right balance of challenge and skill, and a task that truly resonates with you. But when you find it, your mind is wonderfully and spectacularly alive.

5 THINGS IN LIFE THAT ARE HARDER THAN THEY USED TO BE

Patience: Instant gratification culture has made patience harder than ever to cultivate. We want immediate answers, immediate delivery, and immediate access. Intentionally practicing patience builds long-term resilience. It also increases mindfulness and generates a sense of gratitude and contentment. Keep in mind—some things just take time.

Long-form Reading: With information so readily available these days packaged as bite-sized dopamine-bombs, the practice of long-form reading can feel antiquated. Many people prefer quicker, more easily-digestible content over complex articles or lengthy novels. Regular readers, however, cultivate the ability to sustain focus and attention while enriching their lives with beauty, humor, and (hopefully) wisdom.

Privacy: In the age of social media, the concept of privacy is under siege. Many people, particularly younger generations, are comfortable sharing their lives openly on the internet, which can erode our sense of personal privacy. A healthy level of privacy leads to more intimate and close-knit relationships with those who matter most, while oversharing can lead to superficial relationships that feel distant and disconnected.

Focus: In a world of constant notifications and multitasking, the ability to focus on a single task for an extended period can be undermined. This can impact productivity and the quality of work, and can make it harder to engage in deep thought or creative processes. It can also hurt relationships with people as you struggle to stay connected and engaged amidst distraction. Intentionally practicing focus, either through meditation, reading, journaling, or some other exercise where you focus on one thing at a time can make it easier to tap into the well of focus whenever it's needed.

Self-Reliance: With an app or service for almost every modern need, self-reliance can seem a bit outdated. Activities like cooking, navigation, investing, and entertainment can all be easily outsourced to apps designed to make your life easier. AI is making huge strides to help us with all sorts of tasks, both personal and professional. Before you rely too much on those services, however, I suggest learning to do them yourself to a reasonable extent.

BUILDING STRUCTURES FOR CHAOS

I've always been a bit chaotic. My creative energy bursts in every direction, often thrilling, sometimes messy. But chaos, unchecked, can devour itself. I've learned that lesson too many times over the years . . .

I've also learned that building some basic, helpful structures into my life isn't a betrayal of who I am. It's a tool to protect me, to clear the way for my often chaotic self to thrive and create forward momentum in my life rather than simply spinning my tires in the dirt. If you can relate to feeling a bit too chaotic at times, I recommend trying some of the following ideas to build gentle structure into your life without losing your uniquely wonderful independent spirit.

Know and Follow Your North Stars
What are the things in life that matter most to you? What are the ideals you want to move closer to? The goals you wish to achieve? The values you want to uphold? Write down your North Stars and revisit them regularly. Try your best to align your life to those North Stars and let them lead you through the chaos of life.

Keep a Calendar, Even If It's Bare Bones
Don't overdo it, but be consistent. Write down what matters—meetings, deadlines, commitments, helpful reminders. If you don't like feeling so structured, remember that the calendar doesn't control your time; it protects it and shows you where and when you can relax and give time back to yourself. Learning to use a calendar is a means to peace and freedom. Do it, and learn to do it well!

Have a Consistent Place to Write Things Down

When thoughts, tasks, or ideas pop up, *write them down!* I do this in one of three places—my calendar, my journal, or my Notes app. That's it. No scratch paper or sticky notes. If it's important, it goes in one of those landing zones. Once you're in that habit, everything you need is safely written down for later. If you decide later that something's not important, you can always delete it! Regularly review what you've captured. Follow up with the things that matter, and let the rest drift away.

Build a System of Helpful Habits

Over time, build yourself a collection of habits that support your life and goals. Start with things like "I plan my week on Sundays," "I clear out my work email before the weekend," and "I check my planner early and often every day." It's best to build one habit at a time, which can feel like slow progress, but over time your life will become smoother and more fulfilling. One caveat—don't over-program yourself. You're not a machine, so don't treat yourself like one.

Celebrate Your Progress

Chaos thrives on the feeling of *never enough*. Flip that script when something gets done. Pause. Acknowledge that you've done something worthwhile. This silent celebration and self-acknowledgment will keep you coming back for more. We're so hard on ourselves sometimes, so don't forget to be your own biggest fan in those moments you've earned it.

GEARS OF THE MIND

Navigating the complexities of the mind can often feel like mastering the gears of a finely tuned car. Each gear, from idle to redline, represents a different state of mental engagement, varying from serene relaxation to intensely demanding hyper-focus.

By exploring each gear, we can learn to better manage our mental energy, optimize our focus, and maintain a healthier balance between productivity and rest. Additionally, it can help us connect with the people in our lives and build richer, more meaningful relationships.

Let's shift through each gear together:

Neutral | Total Relaxation. Imagine sinking into a soft cloud, floating with no particular direction. It's essential downtime where your mind is free from the constraints of focused activity. This state allows for mental recuperation, fostering creativity and spontaneous thought. In neutral, we can simply be with others—sharing silence, enjoying laughter, or taking in the moment without an agenda. It's the space where connections deepen through shared, peaceful presence.

First Gear / Getting Going. First Gear is a gentle nudge forward—the smooth transition from idleness to motion. It's when your mind starts to engage with the world around you at a leisurely pace. You might be planning your day, contemplating a book you've just read, or simply deciding what to have for breakfast. It's a low-stress state where tasks don't demand much mental horsepower. It's a soft 'good morning' to a loved one, a lingering hug, or the small, thoughtful gestures that let your people know you're thinking about them. BONUS—First gear is also great for "pulling stumps." In other words, if you need to do some seriously challenging work, sometimes "low-and-slow" is the way to go.

Second Gear // Taking It Easy. Second Gear sees a slight increase in mental or physical RPMs. Here you're engaged in routine activities that require a bit more attention but are still within your comfort zone. These tasks are the background music of life—familiar, comforting, and often automatic. In this space, we find shared routines like cooking dinner together, walking side-by-side, or chatting about nothing in particular. It's the gear of effortless companionship and connection amidst the rhythm of daily life. It's the low-and-slow pace that allows you to take in the view. An activity like journaling can be a great "downshifting" activity, slowing yourself to a more relaxed pace after a day at work or a stressful situation.

Third Gear /// Steady as She Goes. Third Gear represents the standard operating level for most of our daily tasks. Your mind is alert and active, capable of multitasking and handling the usual demands of work and life with competence. It's also the gear where we often engage socially—exchanging ideas at work or catching up with a friend over a drink. This is a sweet spot where shared energy leads to a steady, comfortable pace of life. **BONUS**—Third gear is great for climbing hills. When your life feels like an uphill trudge, third gear is a good place to be to make steady progress.

Fourth Gear //// Picking up the Pace. Fourth Gear is when your mental engine really starts to hum. This gear demands more of your mental resources, requiring deeper focus and more complex thought processes. It's the zone of challenging work projects, engaging in deep analytical thought, or learning new skills. Here, relationships can act as a source of energy, or a steadying force. Whether it's leaning on a mentor for insight or collaborating actively towards a common goal, this is the gear where you may need to start managing your energy over extended periods of time.

Fifth Gear ///// High-Speed Performance. Fifth Gear is a controlled sprint. It's when you're fully immersed in a task, with a laser-like focus that blocks out external distractions. This gear is reserved for those moments requiring your utmost attention and effort—think critical decision-making, intense creative bursts, or navigating complex situations. It's exhilarating and can lead to significant breakthroughs, but it's also taxing on your mental resources. In this intense state, the people we trust can become our touchpoints to keep us grounded with check-ins and acknowledgment of their support.

Sixth Gear/Redline ////// Pushing the Limit. Sixth Gear is closing in on the edge of your mental capabilities where you're pushing beyond your typical limits. It's the all-nighter before an exam, the final push on a make-or-break project, or any situation where you're maxing out your mental and/or physical capacity. While this mode of life can lead to moments of extraordinary achievement, it's also where stress and fatigue accumulate the fastest. Operating in this gear should be the exception, not the norm, as it can lead to mental and physical burnout. You can't do this alone for any sustained period of time. Relying on your people is the difference between burnout and breakthrough. An encouraging text from a longtime friend, reassuring words from a spiritual leader, or the support that comes from leaning on your life partner can make all the difference to push through when putting it all on the line.

Shifting Gears. Understanding the "Gears of the Mind" is about recognizing that not every task requires the same level of mental engagement and that shifting gears is a natural and necessary part of maintaining mental well-being and productivity. It's also about recognizing how these mental states influence our relationship with others—when to lean in, when to pull back, and when to simply be together.

By learning to identify which gear is most appropriate for a given task or situation, you can enjoy a healthier, more balanced approach to work, life, and relationships. No matter what, remember that at the end of the day, the greatest journeys we travel are more about the ride than the destination.

CULTIVATING MINDFUL PRESENCE

Mindful presence is a rare superpower in a world full of distractions. However, it may be more accessible than you think.

Start by noticing what's right in front of you. Don't force focus. Just gently pay attention—to the warmth of your coffee mug. The breeze on your skin. The rhythm of the words on this page. When you pause to appreciate small things, life slows down. The moment sharpens. You become present.

When you read, don't rush. Savor the way words flow. It's like finding the groove of a new song by a favorite artist. Between tasks, pause and breathe. Check in with your body. Are you rushing? Is your heart racing? A few deep breaths can help you reset. Try a quick sensory reset: What are five things you see? Four you can touch? Three you hear? Two you smell? One you taste?

Then, think about n o t h i n g.

Feeling anxious or scattered? Upset or riled up? Pause and name your emotions. No judgment—simply notice. Naming them grounds you in the present, acknowledging your current reality. Eating food can even be a mindfulness practice. Don't just eat—savor the textures, notice the flavors, admire the colors. *Pay attention.*

Engage. Dive in. Connect. It's the difference between hearing and listening, between watching and participating, between reading and comprehending. When you fully engage, life becomes more meaningful.

95

In your next conversation, listen like it's the most interesting thing in the world. People notice when you're present, and it makes them feel loved. Focus on one task at a time. Turn off notifications. You'll find you can be more productive while exerting less energy and using less time.

Create no-tech zones during your day—at meals, in the morning, before bed. Engage with what's happening around you. Ask deeper questions in conversations. Listen closely to what people say and respond with kindness and affirmation.

Set a timer for tasks. Focus on one thing for 15, 20, 30 minutes at a time. No multitasking. Full engagement.

When attention and engagement meet, something clicks. It's like standing where two rivers meet—calm yet powerful, steady yet moving.

With practice, you can turn ordinary moments into something special. Mindful presence isn't abstract; it's a practical way to live more fully. Start small. Listen more closely. Focus on one task. Enjoy the details of everyday life.

The more you practice, the more your world shifts toward clarity and meaning.

I think you'll like it.

HELPFUL HINTS FOR DAILY LIVING – RPM – 2006

1. Reevaluate your priorities hourly.
2. Always consider all options.
3. It pays to be early.
4. Carpe Diem—*Seize the day!*
5. Make it happen.
6. Use your head—save your legs.
7. Smile—no negative thoughts.
8. Be happy—and tell your face.
9. Be grateful all day long.
10. Praise the Lord often.
11. Don't postpone joy.
12. Always check your wake.
13. Maintain perfect posture—walk vertical.
14. Drink water often. Don't pass up a water fountain.
15. O-H-I-O = Only Handle It Once to eliminate clutter.
16. When driving, always signal every turn.

Colonel Robert P. Moody (1922-2016)

To me, these words are sacred. This original list, written on a 4x6 note card, was given to me with an encouraging note before I went away for college. It's a distillation of wisdom from a card-carrying member of "The Greatest Generation." I've built much of my personal character upon this list and reference it regularly to remind myself how I'd like to live.

PART 2

ON CHANGE AND GROWING

CATERPILLARS, GOO, AND BUTTERFLIES

I have a theory about growing up. It's messy, unpredictable, and kind of gross, but if you get through it, something amazing happens. Let me explain . . .

The Caterpillar Stage

Kids in elementary school are a lot like caterpillars. They gobble up knowledge as they move around life relatively carefree. It's a time of rapid growth, wobbly first steps, missing teeth, and backpacks that seem at first too big, then too small, for the shoulders they hang on. Kids explore, hungry for knowledge and experience, inching their way through the world, *nom-nom-nomming* everything in their path. They take in incredible amounts of information—words, numbers, friendships, jokes, the unwritten rules of being a human—just to name a few. They don't know (or think about) what they're becoming. They just move forward each and every day, ready for whatever comes their way. The instinct is to fatten themselves up with goodness so they're ready for what comes next . . .

The Goo Phase

If you cut open an actual cocoon mid-process, you won't find a half-formed butterfly with little wings poking out. You'll find goo. The caterpillar actually dissolves itself, breaking down in a soupy, unrecognizable mess before somehow, impossibly, remaking itself into something new.

Including my time as a teacher, I've been in middle school more years than not. I know the goo-phase well. *I was born in it—raised by it!* The chaos is real. One kiddo is having a breakdown because their best friend sat at a different lunch table. Another forgot their locker combination for the hundredth time. A third is about to fail a class but swears they'll turn in their missing work tomorrow. It's messy, it's unpredictable, and it can smell weird. But it's also where magic is happening.

Early in adolescence, people begin to realize that they need to think and act for themselves. They need to decide what type of person they want to be—not because of who their parents or teachers want them to become, but because it's truly who they themselves want to be. *That's an enormous responsibility.* Some kids are ready to make that jump earlier than others, but at some point it's a reality everyone must face. *You yourself control your destiny.* That's pretty wild.

People on the outside often want to try and control the transformation. They quickly find that's an impossible task. Others go the opposite route and want to be completely hands-off. While that may seem like an easy solution, the cocoon still needs protection and love. Even with such a hard protective shell, if the change inside is going to be healthy and good, having a healthy and good environment is ideal. Navigating the goo phase is not easy work. A little bit of positive influence goes a long way.

The Butterfly Phase

When you're in the goo phase, it's almost impossible to believe that something magical is happening. You feel stuck, lost, and like you're falling apart in every possible way. It feels nothing like becoming something new and wonderful. And yet—whether it happens in middle school, high school, or sometime later, the butterfly does emerge. You stretch out, test your wings, and take flight. You've grown, changed, and become something undeniably different from that eager little caterpillar you once were. You may not feel fully formed yet, but there is a newfound freedom in simply being you. You are ready for whatever adventures and challenges come your way.

At first, flying through this stage of life is exhilarating. There's nothing quite like the feeling of doing something that once seemed impossible. You gain independence, make choices that shape your future, and begin stepping into the person you want to become. Some butterflies take off immediately, soaring boldly into the unknown. Others flap awkwardly at first, unsure of where to go or how to get there. No matter how fast or slow it happens, you will emerge, transformed, and everything will be different.

That's not to say this stage is easy—it's not. With freedom comes responsibility, failure, and self-doubt. You may not trust yourself from the get-go, and that's okay. Personally, I've dealt with imposter syndrome and anxiety as I learn to genuinely appreciate my strengths and honestly accept my weaknesses. At 37 years old, I am still learning that I am exactly who I am meant to be, and that I am worthy of unconditional self-love.

It takes time to build trust in your new self, figuring out how to maneuver in a world that's suddenly bigger, less structured, and filled with endless possibilities. Where once we were safely confined, now we are fully open to the experiences life has to offer, for better and for worse.

We Don't Stop Transforming

One flaw with this whole analogy is that human children are not in fact caterpillars, and human adults are not in fact butterflies. We're humans. And as humans, we don't just transform once. Life is going to throw you back into a cocoon at least a few more times. Things like marriage, hardship, tragedy, parenthood—these things will rock your world and you *will* change. The truth is, you will continue to transform in new and wonderful ways throughout your entire life.

I'm in the middle of a pretty messy goo phase in my life right now as my wife and I raise our two daughters, now 2 and 4 years old. It's been a lot like those middle school days all over again—awkward, frustrating, challenging—but also magical. My wife and I are learning to trust each other, ourselves, and the support systems we've built over the years.

Whether you are in a transformation stage or spreading your wings and flying freely, continue to nourish your mind, body, and spirit. What you take in today will help you grow into what you're meant to become. So read good books. Eat good food. Drink water. Foster healthy relationships with people you care about. Take care of yourself, and help take care of others. For when the next goo phase comes—and it will—you'll need a good amount of strength, wisdom, and love stored up to carry you through. And on the other side? You'll emerge once more, new in ways you never expected. But still, unmistakably and wonderfully, *you.*

IN DEFENSE OF TRYING HARD

We learn best by doing, plain and simple. Every time we throw ourselves into something, whether we ace it or face-plant, we're moving forward. Each full-effort rep builds resilience, pumps up our mental strength, and boosts confidence. Plus, when we're giving our best, we tend to unlock hidden jolts of creativity. For all of these reasons, trying hard is a good way to go through life—contrary to what 'cool culture' may tell you.

Giving effort demands vulnerability. Being vulnerable takes guts. But showing up, time and again and putting your best foot forward builds a steady, deep sense of fulfillment and self-esteem. It's easy to fall asleep at night knowing you gave a good, strong effort that day.

Another thing: effort is contagious. When others see you giving your all, it lights a fire in them, too. And here's the kicker—consistent effort means that when the right opportunity knocks, you'll be ready. You've been gearing up for it the whole time without even realizing it. So go, be bold, and do your best. You owe it to yourself and the ones who love you.

A few considerations:

Balance is key. Yes, push yourself, but don't forget to enjoy the ride. Over-exerting yourself for long periods of time can take the fun out of your day-to-day, turning your one wild and precious life into a tedious grind. Your worth isn't measured by how many checkboxes you tick off each day, and sometimes it's okay to say *"&@*# productivity."*

105

You won't always win. Sometimes, even when you've gone all out, the result won't be what you wanted. That's a tough pill to swallow, but the pride of effort doesn't hinge on success. Learn to face disappointments with grace and dignity. It will earn you respect.

Avoid the comparison game. Some days you'll give 110% and still watch someone else breeze by with half the effort. It will feel like you're a stubby little armadillo trying to outrun a cheetah. It's not a fair race! Learn to focus on *your* path, *your* growth, and forget the rest. Comparison is a thief of joy.

BE THE CHANGE—RIGHT HERE, RIGHT NOW

It's easy to feel like the world's problems are too big, too complicated, and too overwhelming. Real change, however, doesn't start with grand gestures—it starts with small, meaningful choices. If something feels off, neglected, or in need of care, the most powerful question to ask is, "What can I do?"

You don't have to fix everything. The world is complex, and no one person can do it all. But your home, your community, your workplace—these *are* places where your efforts can make a real difference.

Small actions matter. Listening when someone needs support. Organizing a space to make life easier. Showing up when it counts. These moments shape the world around you. And when enough people take responsibility for their own little corner, the whole world is a better place.

It's tempting to wait for the right time, the right resources, or for someone else to take the lead. But change doesn't require perfection. It just requires quiet consistency. Even a small step forward, each and every day, creates steady progress. That's how I wrote this book! Start taking consistent action toward the change you want to see and people will begin to take notice.

And they don't just notice—they'll start to follow your lead. Your kids, your coworkers, your friends—when they see you stepping up, it encourages them to do the same.

If you want to see something shift in your life—at work, in a relationship, on a team, with your health—whatever it is, don't wait around. Be the change. Start right here. Start right now. *Let's get specific. Here's how it might look . . .*

. . . In the Workplace

A simple *"Hey, I saw what you did there—nice work!"* can turn someone's day around and spark a better vibe for everyone. If the culture is dragging, take it upon yourself to lift it up. One person, with consistent action, can make a difference. Remember—leadership doesn't have to come from the top.

. . . On a Team

Try to keep the team's goals ahead of your own. If people are slipping into negativity or focusing solely on "me" instead of "we," be the person who brings everyone back to the table to remind them you're all working toward the same goal.

. . . With Relationships

Want more joy, fun, honesty, or spontaneity? *Bring it!* Sometimes you have to start dancing before someone wants to join you. Don't worry about looking goofy— that's where the fun is. Want to have more meaningful conversations? Ask better questions. Create space for one-on-one connections. Stop waiting for it to happen, and just do it.

. . . With Friends

Feel like the crew isn't as tight as it used to be? Make the first move. Be the friend who shows up. Be the friend who keeps the conversation going and helps make plans happen. The rest just may follow your lead.

. . . With Your Health

Start with small steps like choosing healthier foods, incorporating physical activity, and prioritizing rest. Also, develop a habit to nurture your mental well-being. Journaling is my go-to but other options (meditation, quiet time) can be helpful too.

SOME CONTRADICTIONS OF GROWING UP

Be brave, but know when to ask for help.
Be confident, but stay humble.
Be open-minded, but stay rooted in your core beliefs.
Be prepared, but stay flexible.
Be yourself, but learn to fit in.
Chase your passions, but live responsibly.
Do your best, but don't show off.
Plan for the future, but live in the moment.
Honor the past, but strive for a better future.

TAMING YOUR DEMONS >>> INDULGING THEM

We all have demons—simmering frustrations, flashes of anger, moments of shame. They lurk, whispering from the depths of our minds, urging us to say the things we shouldn't, do the things that feel good in the moment but leave us feeling empty. Indulging our demons can *feel* powerful. Think of slamming your hand on the horn when someone cuts you off. It's immediate, raw, and primal. There's the thrill, but it fades fast, leaving you emptier than before.

Now . . . taming those demons? That's a whole different kind of power. Stepping back when you want to jump forward, breathing deep when your chest is burning, and making what you know is the right choice even when nobody's watching. When you manage to do that—to take urges you know are counterproductive and shape them into something good—it's incredibly satisfying. It's not about denying who you are or pretending you're flawless; it's about consistently striving to be a person you yourself are proud of.

It isn't easy work. But after the moment of truth, you'll look back and see moments where you could've let your demons run wild, and instead you'll find peace. In place of the chaos and darkness you could've unleashed in your life, you'll find strength, satisfaction, and a version of yourself that fills you with pride.

And it will all be worth it.

DEALING WITH RACING THOUGHTS

I had a vision last night that may be helpful for people who, like me, experience racing thoughts from time to time.

Having racing thoughts is the unsettling sensation of ideas blasting through your consciousness faster than you can process them.

For me, this causes an out-of-control type of anxiety that makes it hard to function in any meaningful way beyond the simplest tasks. It's overwhelming and can even feel a bit scary at times.

Last night, as I lay in bed with racing thoughts, I visualized my racing thoughts as literal race cars blowing past me at the start/finish line at the Indianapolis 500.

Nyyeeee-roooooom!

Nyyeeee-roooooom!

Nyyeeee-roooooom!

I'm not a big racing fan, but stick with me . . .

In my mind, I tried to focus on just a single car—a single idea—as it raced past.

When my consciousness locked on to one of these cars/ideas, I mentally got in the driver's seat and gained control of that particular car/idea.

When I started taking control of ideas one by one, I realized most simply weren't important to me at that moment.

Some weren't even rational.

With patience and a bit of (imagined) skill, I simply pulled many ideas onto pit road, parking them in a garage.

A few ideas weren't even worthy of a spot in my mental "garage," so I just let those cars smash into the wall and disappear into a ball of flames.

It didn't take long for the racetrack to clear and for my mind to relax.

The last idea I remember focusing on last night was very simple:

I need to sleep.

I drove that car steadily through the empty oval until I drifted off into peaceful rest.

WHY IS IT SO HARD TO SIMPLY DO LESS?

Cutting back or doing less can feel like an impossible task, especially when life pulls you in a thousand directions every day. There's a constant pressure to keep going—to always be on top of everything, even when you know deep down that something has to give. It's not just about having too much on your plate. It runs far deeper. The struggle to simply do less is tied to how we see ourselves. It connects to what we think the world expects from us. It has to do with the inner battles we fight through the different phases of life.

We want to do less, but it can feel like a near-impossible ask. *Why is that?*

Being busy makes us feel valued. Many of us equate a packed schedule with importance and success. However, this leads us to seek validation through being busy, which can trap us in endless cycles of commitments. Recognizing that your worth isn't defined by how much you do is key to finding more meaningful engagement in fewer, more fulfilling activities.

It's hard to say no. Often, we struggle with saying no because we fear missing out or disappointing others. But learning to say no is crucial—it means we're actually saying yes to things that are more important to us. It's about prioritizing what truly matters over just being busy.

We put a lot of pressure on ourselves. We often face internal pressures to make the 'right' decisions, achieve perfection, or meet every expectation. But there isn't always a clear or perfect answer. Embracing imperfection and accepting that it's okay to not have everything figured out can help alleviate these pressures, making it easier to manage our commitments and reduce our load.

We feel pressure from others, real and imagined. We've all experienced the fear of missing out—that nagging feeling that something important will pass you by if you slow down. It's hard to slow down while the world keeps rushing by, urging you to do more, be more, in more ways, to more people. But the truth is, when we spread ourselves too thin, we lose the strength and ability to be our best selves when it matters most.

Learning to cut back the overgrowth from your life is hard and takes time, but it's worth it. When you learn to let go, you'll begin to realize that the things you thought you'd lose—value, purpose, belonging—don't go anywhere after all. In many cases, those things will feel stronger than they had before, now that your commitments better align with your goals, values, and personal well-being.

Give yourself permission to say no.

There may be consequences.

But what are the consequences of the status quo?

WHAT SUCCESS MIGHT LOOK LIKE AT AGE . . .

. . . 1
[Giggles and claps hands]
[Eats a bite of food with a fork]
[Takes first steps]
"Mama! Dada!"
[Falls asleep after a lullaby]

. . . 4
"I found a bug!"
"I buttoned my pants!"
"Watch me jump!"
"I shared my cookie with a friend!"
"I spelled my name!"

. . . 8
"I was brave at the doctor's office."
"I read a whole chapter book."
"My bedroom looks really nice."
"I learned how to play a song on the piano."
"I stood up for my friend during recess."

. . . 13
"I made the school soccer team."
"I'm learning to play guitar."
"I volunteered at a food bank."
"I babysat my cousins and everyone had a blast."
"I can do the laundry."

. . . 16
"I passed my driver's test."
"I saved up money and bought my own computer."
"I'm getting good grades."
"I got a part in the musical."
"We went on a date."

. . . 18
"I have some really great friends."
"I got into college and my mom cried happy tears."
"I voted for the first time."
"I'm learning to cook."
"I have a credit card."

. . . ???

_____

_____

_____

_____

_____

PART 3

ON LOVE, LOSS, AND THE PASSAGE OF TIME

STOP SEEING LIFE AS A THING TO DO . . .

. . . and start seeing life as a time to love.

Love your God, love your neighbor, love yourself.

That shift changes everything.

Love isn't just a sweet feeling or a spark that flares up when things are going well. Love is an active choice—a ready posture of the spirit and soul. It's the willingness to take time and energy to nurture a relationship. It's being kind to others and yourself. It's doing the things necessary to make the world a better place.

This means waking up each day ready to show up for the people in your life, even if you're tired or busy.

It means giving yourself grace and honoring your own personal boundaries, because you are worthy of your own love and respect.

It means living not for your to-do list, but understanding that your life holds more meaning and purpose than just productivity.

Sacrifice is part of the equation, but choosing love is not about losing yourself. It's about finding yourself in the giving. The magic of selfless love is that it fills our own tanks as well. Choosing love is the ultimate win-win. And when we make that choice day in and day out, season after season, what awaits is a beautiful surprise . . .

Joy.

Real, lasting, *joy.*

THE DANCE

Married life is a dance. Not the polished ballroom kind that you shared during the first dance at your wedding, but more like navigating a crowded dance floor where you sometimes lead, sometimes follow, and often trip over your partner's feet.

We all want our lives to run smoothly and for our plans to fall in place without too much friction. But just when you're expecting to hit a steady groove, life often switches tempo, leaving you and your loved ones scrambling to catch up.

The nice thing about this dance is that it's not about perfection; it's about connection. You don't have to hit each step exactly right. This dance is impossible to choreograph in advance because we have no idea what the band is going to play as the night goes on. But if you tune in to your partner throughout the night, work on your rhythm and coordination, and laugh together at the missteps, you'll be able to get through the more chaotic moments and find your stride once more.

Keep paying attention. Keep working together. Practice leading and practice being led. Over time, you'll get a better feel for when to spin and when to dip, when to lead, and when to follow.

And if you ever feel lost or alone, just find your partner's eyes in the crowd, bring them close, and sway. Just sway.

Sometimes that's the best we can do.

PARENTING A CHILD WITH A DISABILITY

Being a good parent to a child with a disability is, in my experience, not incredibly different from being a good parent to any other child.

The key is to love, support, and advocate—to learn alongside them as they navigate whatever comes their way. To be a steady force of support and guidance, all wrapped in a blanket of unconditional love.

That being said, here are some pieces of advice I've found helpful specifically for parenting a child with a disability.

Educate yourself about the disability. Learning as much as you can about your child's disability will help you understand their needs and how to best support them. Make the most of opportunities to talk to their doctors, therapists, and other professionals. Write questions down ahead of time so you're ready in the moment. Also, don't hesitate to do your own research to learn more about their condition. Don't go overboard, but it's good to keep learning.

Communicate with your child. Keep the lines of communication open with your child. Talk to them about their feelings, thoughts, and experiences, and listen to what they have to say. This will help you better understand their perspective and how you can support them.

Advocate for your child. If your child needs accommodations or support at school or in other settings, it's important to advocate for them. This might mean working with their teachers or other professionals to make sure they have the resources and support they need to succeed. It's important to respect professionals, but at the same time, nobody knows your child like you. When the time comes, be ready to speak up! I'm not suggesting becoming a "Helicopter" or "Lawnmower" parent, but there's still a level of advocacy that is appropriate and warranted.

Encourage independence. Support your child, but also encourage independence. It builds confidence and life skills that will serve them well. This will look different from person to person, but it's always worth the time and effort. Gaining independence, whatever that looks like, is always a huge deal.

Lean on your village. It's okay to ask for help. When things get really hard—and they will—understand that reaching out to a friend or family member when you're at a low point is not a sign of weakness, but rather a signal of trust. You'll find out who you can count on and who you can't, and the right people will get such joy from helping you through.

Show your love and support. Above all, it's important to let your child know that you love and support them no matter what. Show them, with your words and actions, that you believe in them and that you are there for them. Encourage them to pursue their dreams and passions. Part of this means not always dwelling on their struggles—give space and energy for them to develop their unique gifts, talents, and interests. Don't let a constant desire to improve weaknesses take away from the chance to build on strengths.

This is not a complete or perfect list, but at the end of the day, if we err on the side of love, that should take care of pretty much everything.

P.S. — *CJ, if you're reading this, I love you!* 😊

THE FIVE LOVE DESTROYERS

I can't count how many times I've heard Gary Chapman's "Five Love Languages" come up in my life over the last 15 years. I first heard it in pre-marriage counseling back in 2011. It has come up in lunchroom banter more than a few times. My wife and I occasionally remind each other that we actually enjoy *all* of the love languages.

Recently I found myself wondering if there is a flip-side to each love language. A dark side. Not exactly hate-languages—more like anti-loving behaviors that quietly erode connection over time. Here's my take on what I call "The Five Love Destroyers."

Neglectful Silence/Criticism (Words of Affirmation)
Encouraging words lift people up. No secret there. But what if those words never come? Or if instead of warmth, we sling sharp criticism and scorn? Silence can bruise just as deeply as a harsh insult. It leaves your partner feeling invisible or belittled.

Inattention/Absence (Quality Time)
There's no shortcut for simply being there. Intentional time together can ground and strengthen a relationship. But when we're physically or mentally checked out? It's like saying, "You don't matter." Over time, that distance stacks up, making your partner feel alone, even when they're right next to you.

Withholding/Thoughtlessness (Gift-Giving)
A gift doesn't need a designer label to say "I care." It's about the thought behind it. When we skip important moments or hand over gifts with zero attention or

heart, we send the wrong message. It's easy for a partner to feel cast aside or overlooked when gifts lose the heart behind them, even if they are expensive or showy.

Neglect/Laziness (Acts of Service)

Love in action can speak louder than any words. Helping with the chores, pitching in more during stressful times—that's how we show up. But if we're constantly too busy, too stressed, or just plain can't be bothered, it can feel like we're shrugging off our partner's needs. The message that sends? *You're on your own!* Yeesh. Not good.

Coldness/Physical Distance (Physical Touch)

Touch can fill the gaps when words fall short. A hug, a hand on the shoulder, a gentle kiss—these simple gestures say, "I'm here for you." But when affection is withheld, especially if physical touch is your partner's key love language, it can create not only a physical chasm, but an emotional one too, leaving them starved for connection.

Recognizing the "five love destroyers" isn't just about avoiding what hurts—it's an invitation to lean into what heals. Be present. Be gentle. Be thoughtful. Whether you're just starting out or nurturing a long-term bond, shining a light on these flip-sides can help you steer clear of trouble and keep the love-light burning strong.

SOME THINGS I'VE LEARNED ABOUT GRIEF

The traditional model of the "stages of grief," first presented by Elisabeth Kübler-Ross in her 1969 book *On Death and Dying*, is often thought of as a linear progression. What I've discovered in my own experience of grief is that the journey through these "stages" can be unpredictable. Knowing that has helped me recognize grief when it comes and respond in ways that feel (or at least aim to be) healthy.

Here are my experiences with the five stages of grief.

Denial: Also called "Initial Shock" or "Disbelief," denial involves a sense of numbness about the loss. It's a natural defense mechanism that buffers the immediate shock of a tragedy or loss. I've had feelings of denial come and go throughout the grieving process, often resurfacing at unexpected times when, for whatever reason, I'm unable to acknowledge the new reality I'm in.

Anger: An intense frustration sometimes bordering on rage, my anger emerges in various forms. It has been directed toward different entities including friends, family, God, and even myself. Like denial, anger can appear sporadically throughout the grief journey, rearing its ugly head when I least expect it. Triggers for anger are hard to see coming, and snapping out of that anger state is easier said than done. I've found writing to be a good outlet for my anger, even if it doesn't go anywhere. Just getting my thoughts out can help clarify my feelings and help me get back on track. Listening to music can be a big help too.

Bargaining: Bargaining has shown up for me mostly as wishing things could have been different for one reason or another. It's my way of grappling with the situation and, I think, helps give me some sense of power during hopeless moments. *If only I had done this. If only I hadn't done that. If I go to church every week then God will come to the rescue* . . . Looking back, it looks a lot like false hope. It's a sad place to be, really, which is perhaps why it sometimes leads toward depression.

Depression: In the context of grief, depression is deep sadness that feels hopeless and lonely. It can be pervasive, but for me it tends to come in waves. Periods of intense sadness are interspersed with times of relative normalcy. Feeling this way doesn't mean you're a weak person—but feeling depressed does make you feel weak sometimes, and that's okay. Grief takes a toll.

Acceptance: Acceptance doesn't mean everything is okay. It's more about acknowledging a new reality and recognizing the need to keep moving forward. This stage might never be fully complete, and a person can move in and out of acceptance as time goes on. There will be days I feel more or less at peace with the loss—and that feeling shifts, sometimes day to day, sometimes season to season.

Grief comes in many forms, but one constant it seems is that grieving is hard. If you're a person who has grieved, or will ever grieve, I hope these words help you through the journey in some way.

IN DEFENSE OF SETTLING

In our relentless pursuit of excellence, we're often captivated by the siren song of ambition, constantly encouraged to reach further, dream bigger, and never settle. This mindset, while inspiring, paints a somewhat incomplete picture of personal fulfillment. Today, I want to explore a concept that seems almost heretical in our hyper-ambitious society—the genuine value of settling.

Before you dismiss the idea, hear me out. This is not a call for complacency or an argument to abandon your aspirations. Rather, it's an invitation to immerse yourself in the dance of life unfolding around you. It's an invitation to embrace the beauty of the present moment. An invitation to be at peace.

Here are three potentially healthy ways to settle:

Settle into a Routine. Routine is often written off as a monotonous creativity killer. Another way to view it, however, is the steady rhythm of days, weeks, months, and years that build a strong foundation for a flourishing life. Psychological research suggests that routines anchor our lives, provide a sense of control, and bolster our mental health. Consider the idea of settling into a healthy routine not as a constraint, but as establishing a steady bassline to your life's song, offering you something reliable to improvise above.

Settle into a Job or Career. In a culture fascinated by the new and the next, the idea of longevity in a job might seem quaint, perhaps even obsolete. Yet, there's undeniable value in growing roots within a career. Settling into a job isn't about forgoing ambition; it's about deepening your impact, mastering your craft, and building lasting relationships. It's the difference between skimming the surface and diving deep to discover the treasures that lie beneath. The grass is not always greener, and settling into a job you're succeeding in can open up opportunities for growth in other areas of your life.

Settle into a New Season of Life. Life unfolds in seasons, each with its own tempo and lessons. A few seasons I've experienced so far include childhood, adolescence, early adulthood, and early parenthood. While it's healthy to set goals for ourselves and to always move forward, relentlessly rushing toward the future—or clinging to past seasons we need to release—can blind us to the beauty of now. Buddhism teaches the art of presence—to live in the moment, fully and wholeheartedly. By settling into the current season of your life, you're not giving up on tomorrow; you're honoring the journey, acknowledging that this season of life, with its joys and challenges, is precious and worthy of appreciation.

In conclusion, "settling" need not be a dirty word. Settling doesn't mean shrinking your dreams. It means anchoring them. Take time to reflect: *Where in your life might settling actually feel like arriving? What parts of your world are already good, even if imperfect?*

Part of the journey is accepting imperfections and understanding that good things take time.

And when/if the time comes to move on—you move on.

140

THE INFINITE WITHIN

Something inside each of us hints at the infinite. Our dreams. Our hopes. Our imaginations. The endless well of love we draw from for family and friends.

We sense this limitlessness inside ourselves, but when we try to understand it or harness it, we fall short.

It's as if we're given a fleeting glimpse every now and again into an eternal landscape, but the window we peer through is smeared with the fog of human limitations.

Our dreams, hopes, and even that inexhaustible well of love are all echoes of something greater, reverberating from a distance we can't quite measure. We desperately want to comprehend that "something more," but we're reminded, sometimes painfully and frustratingly so, of our limited vantage point. Our scope, while not insignificant, is like looking through a pinhole at the unimaginable magnitude of it all.

And while our perspective may be small, it is not meaningless; it's the lens through which we engage with this life. And maybe, just maybe, it's designed that way for a reason. It keeps us humble, hungry for truth, and forever seeking to align with that greater plan of glory, even if we only see flashes of it in our lifetime.

Let those flashes of light—those glorious sparks of infinite understanding—intrigue you, inspire you, and fill you with hope.

LIFE IS A MOMENT

Life is a moment we share with every person who ever was, every person who is now, and every person who will ever be.

May we always fill this moment with things that bring us joy and things that bring joy to the ones we love. May we be good to this life, and in return may this life be good to us.

Thank you for being here with me.

ABOUT THE AUTHOR

Most people around town know me as "Mr. Moody," the middle school teacher. *Fun fact:* the middle school I attended—Jones Middle School—was named for my great-grandfather, J.W. Jones. You could say middle school is in my blood.

I enjoyed a fairly typical late-nineteen-hundreds Midwest upbringing. I had two loving and supportive parents, a great role model for an older brother, two dogs, two gerbils, two goldfish, a turtle named Hot Shot, iconic grandparents, a dozen-or-so trophies, and wonderful friends just about every step of the way.

If there was one thing that defined my childhood, it's that I played. A lot. Like, *a lot* a lot.

My favorite toys were Legos, Hot Wheels cars, and the family camcorder. My brother and I spent hundreds of hours recording on that thing. I've also always enjoyed computer and video games. One thing I've come to appreciate in life is the importance of play—at any age.

If there's been one defining characteristic of my whole life, it's that *people have believed in me*. My teachers, my family, my friends, my students, my colleagues, my bosses, you name it . . . they've laughed with me, trusted me, supported me, and empowered me. This village of mine is something special, and it began with my mom and dad.

My mom has the most beautiful soul. She cares more deeply than anyone I've known. She is fiercely proud of her family and has given so much of herself to us all. She is an incredible cook. Everything she makes tastes wonderful, and she really can do it all. The most impressive part is that she rarely uses a recipe. She is an artist in nearly every aspect of her life.

My dad is also an excellent cook but usually sticks to smoking meats and making breakfast. He also makes fantastic sandwiches. Dads make excellent sandwiches. My dad taught me the importance of details—of doing the job well and of returning a borrowed tool in better condition than you found it. An architect by trade and a creator at heart, he has a gift of bringing beauty into simple, everyday existence.

Both of my parents are skilled artists and free spirits. They are dedicated, loyal, and hard-working. Mom and Dad—you have always loved me well, and I want nothing more than to make you proud. Thank you for everything. A big shout-out as well to my brother Paul. You've been a powerful inspiration to me and I've always appreciated your kindness, inclusiveness, and generosity.

Next, I want to share a bit about my incredible wife, Anna. Anna—through thick and thin, you have been by my side, my most steadfast supporter and constant companion. We've been through a lot together, and you've somehow come to know me better than I know myself. Perhaps the greatest gift you've given me is your dedication to faith and family that is now ingrained on my soul. Thank you for being you and for loving me for me.

Finally, my daughters. My beautiful daughters. Charlotte and Olivia—you are the reason I try each day to live as well as I can. I hope to make this world a better place for you, as you have made this world a better place for me. *Shine on, my little loves, shine on!*

To all the rest reading this—there is nothing more precious than time, and I hope you found the time we shared on these pages well-spent. I'd love to hear from you about which poems, stories, and blurbs you enjoyed the most. Message me at **thewritermoody@gmail.com** and let me know. Once again—thank you for being here.

REFLECTION QUESTIONS — POEMS

❖ **"Little Bird"** (p.7) is about love, protection, and the bittersweet feeling of watching someone grow up. Who or what in your life feels like a little bird—something precious you want to protect, nurture, and set free? Why is it often important to let go of the things or people we love?

❖ **"Awake"** (p.9) captures the energy of spring and the feeling of renewal. It reminds us that change can bring both excitement and beauty into our lives. Think about a time in your life when things felt fresh and new. Do some writing about that time. What made that time special? Who was there with you? How are things different now than they were before?

❖ The speaker in **"Love Me Whole"** (p.11) longs for love to make them feel complete. It raises the question of whether love is something we find within ourselves or in the people around us. What does it mean to truly love someone? What does it mean to truly love yourself? Does love come from within, or from the relationships we build?

❖ Some objects carry deep meaning because they remind us of people we love and what they stood for. **"Paw Paw's Hat"** (p.13) reflects on how simple things can hold powerful memories. What are some objects that remind you of family members or other people you love? What memories do you associate with some of those objects?

❖ The poem **"Set Sail"** (p.15) compares life and love to a journey at sea. It suggests that love can serve as a guiding force through both calm waters and storms. If your life were a journey at sea, where do you feel you are right now? Who is on the ship with you? What challenges have you navigated together and what have you learned from them? What are you journeying toward together?

* "**Charlotte's Song**" (p.17) tells a story of struggle, faith, and strength in the face of hardship. It reflects on how love and resilience can carry us through even the most difficult moments. Can you think of a time when you or someone you know had to stay strong through a difficult season? What helped you keep going? What role do faith and hope play in getting through the hardest times?

* Everyone needs guidance at different points in life, whether from people, beliefs, or personal experiences. "**Guiding Light**" (p.19) explores what helps us find our way when we feel lost. Who or what helps you feel grounded when life is confusing or difficult? How do they guide you?

* The poem "**Folks**" (p.21) describes the kinds of people who make the world better through simple acts of kindness. It reminds us to notice and appreciate those who quietly care for others. Think of someone in your life who fits this description. How do they inspire you? What small acts of kindness can a person do to make the world around them better?

* "**Glory Be to Us All**" (p.23) celebrates the overlooked and the ordinary, reminding us that everyone has worth. It wrestles with the idea of feeling worthy of love even when we see ourselves as broken, ugly, or 'less than'. Why do you think some people struggle with self-love? Reflect on how, in hindsight, your challenges, struggles, or scars are worthy of celebration.

* "**A Thousand Minds**" (p.25) explores what it feels like to have endless thoughts racing through your head. What do you do when your thoughts feel overwhelming? How do you find calm in a busy mind? What situations might come up where having many thoughts or ideas can be helpful?

❖ People often shape themselves to fit the world around them. The poem **"Wax Folk"** (p.27) raises questions about whether change is always necessary, and when it might be better to stay true to oneself. Why do people try to change themselves for others? When is change a good thing, and when is it not?

❖ **"The Boy and the King"** (p.29) is about forgiveness, even in the most difficult moments. It reminds us that sometimes, letting go of anger can be more powerful than holding onto it. Why do you think forgiveness is so hard? Why do you think forgiveness is so powerful? Who is impacted more by forgiveness—the person being forgiven or the person doing the forgiving?

❖ This poem **"Your Death"** (p.31) expresses grief and the deep love that remains after loss. It reminds us that love does not disappear, even when someone is gone. How do you keep the memory of important people in your life? What does it look like to make the most of the time you have with the ones you love?

❖ "**Peace Be with You**" (p.33) follows someone from childhood to old age, offering peace at every stage of life. It reminds us that peace is something we can seek at every step of our journey. What does "peace" mean to you? Where have you found it? In what stages of life do you think it's easiest and most difficult to find peace?

REFLECTION QUESTIONS — STORIES

❖ In the story "**Jamie's Garden**" (p.37) the main character dedicates years to transforming a plot of land that others see as worthless. His story is about perseverance, believing in something when no one else does, and the slow but meaningful process of growth. What is something in your life that you've worked hard on, even when others doubted it? How did you stay motivated? How do you know when something is truly worth working for, even when progress is slow?

❖ In **"Benny's First Forage"** (p.43) Benny is excited to explore the world and find food on his own, but he also faces fear and unexpected challenges. His journey reflects the excitement of independence and the importance of loving guidance. Think about a time when you had to do something on your own for the first time. How did you feel before, during, and after? Who has helped you on your journey toward independence?

❖ Throughout the story **"Sorry, Honey"** (p.47) young Lenore is eager for her parents' attention, but they are too distracted to notice. This story explores the quiet pain of feeling unseen and what happens when love and connection are put on hold. At what points in your life have you felt unheard or overlooked? Why do you think people sometimes get too distracted to notice what really matters? How can we be more present for the people in our lives?

❖ In the story **"Robbie the Robot"** (p.55) Robbie discovers he can control how much he focuses on others versus how much he focuses on himself. By the end of the story, he learns that balance—between giving and taking care of yourself—is the key to feeling whole. How do you balance helping others with taking care of yourself? What happens when someone gives too much without setting limits? How can we support others while maintaining our own well-being?

❖ **"A Bargain"** (p.63) tells the story of a desperate artist who trades a part of herself for success, believing it will bring her happiness. Over time, she realizes what she gave up was more valuable than what she gained. This story raises the question of what we are willing to sacrifice for achievement—and whether it is always worth the cost. What does "success" in life mean to you? How is your definition of success similar to or different from society's definition of success? What signs might indicate that you are giving up too much to pursue success?

❖ **"The Ballad of Willard McFee"** (p.71) shares the whimsical story of a sailor lost at sea. That sailor drifts far away from where he wants to be and ends up trapped in a cave far below the surface of the ocean. Willard McFee teaches us about holding on to hope and the power of love to withstand the test of time. What advice would you give a person who finds they've drifted far away from the life they want for themselves? Who are the people you love so much you would wait decades to return to them?

REFLECTION QUESTIONS — BLURBS PT 1

❖ **"6 Things Everyone Can and Should Do"** (p.79) highlights six simple but important practices that can lead to a more meaningful and fulfilling life. It reminds us that small, consistent actions—like kindness and gratitude—can have a big impact. Which of these six ideas do you already practice? Which one do you want to work on?

❖ **"A Lesson in Character"** (p.81) reminds us that character is not about appearances but about choices—especially the ones no one else sees. It explores how integrity is built over time, one decision at a time. Who is someone you admire for their character? What do they do that sets them apart?

❖ **"Flow: The Heart of Focus"** (p.83) describes the feeling of being so engaged in something that time disappears. This state of flow is a sign that you're doing something that matters—and that fits you well. When was the last time you experienced flow? What were you doing, and why did it matter? What kinds of activities make time fly for you, and how can you build more of them into your life?

❖ **"5 Things That Are Harder Than They Used to Be"** (p.87) reflects on how daily habits like patience, focus, and presence have become harder to maintain in a distracted world. It invites us to consider how we can reclaim these foundational skills. Which of these challenges do you struggle with the most? Why do you think that is?

❖ **"Building Structures for Chaos"** (p.89) points out that we can't always control what happens, but we can build habits and systems to help us stay grounded. When chaos comes, structure is what keeps us steady. Do you tend to be more structured or more chaotic? How does that affect your day-to-day life? What's one habit or routine that helps you feel more grounded when life feels unpredictable?

❖ **"Gears of the Mind"** (p.91) compares mental states to shifting gears in a car—some days we cruise, and some days we grind. It suggests that learning to shift gears intentionally can help us live and work better. What "gear" do you feel like you're usually in? Is that where you want to be? At what times of day could you intentionally shift your mind's gears?

❖ **"Cultivating Mindful Presence"** (p.95) encourages us to slow down and truly notice the moment we're in. It reminds us that life happens in the present—not in a past we regret or a future we worry about. What's one small way you can practice being more present today? How does technology help—or hurt—your ability to be present in the moment?

❖ **"Helpful Hints for Daily Living – RPM 2006"** (p.97) offers life wisdom passed down from a previous generation—short sayings with deep truths. These simple tips remind us to care for ourselves and others with grace and common sense. Which pieces of advice stand out most to you? Why? If you had to write your own "helpful hints" for future generations, what would be on your list?

REFLECTION QUESTIONS — BLURBS PT 2

❖ **"Caterpillars, Goo, and Butterflies"** (p.101) uses the life cycle of a butterfly as a metaphor for how we grow and change. Each stage has its purpose, even the ones that feel slow, quiet, or painful. Do you feel like you're in a caterpillar, cocoon, or butterfly stage right now? Why? What would you say to someone who's in the middle of a long, hard waiting season?

❖ **"In Defense of Trying Hard"** (p.105) makes the case for effort, even when it's not rewarded or recognized. It argues that there's nothing more honest or beautiful than giving your all. Have you ever felt judged for giving too much effort or for caring too much about something? Why do some people act like trying hard is somehow uncool? How much effort is too much effort?

❖ **"Be the Change—Right Here, Right Now"** (p.107) reminds us that we don't have to change the whole world—we just have to start where we are. Real change often begins with something small and close to home. Of the places listed, where might you consider being the change? What kind of change do you hope to see? What might it look like to start making these changes?

❖ **"Some Contradictions of Growing Up"** (p.111) reflects on how growing up means learning to hold two truths at once: strength and softness, freedom and responsibility, confidence and doubt. It asks us to live in the tension, not run from it. What's a contradiction from this list you've experienced in your own growth? How have you learned to hold both sides of it?

* **"Taming Your Demons >>> Indulging Them"** (p.113) reminds us that we all experience temptations, but we also have the ability to resist them. This piece challenges us to face our patterns instead of letting them lead us. How is "taming your demons" different from running from your demons? Is it ever helpful to ignore or deny a problem? Who or what might help you overcome your strongest temptations?

* **"Dealing with Racing Thoughts"** (p.115) describes the feeling of being stuck in your own head, unable to slow down. It offers a gentle reminder that you're not alone, and that there are ways to find calm again. What do you do when your thoughts feel overwhelming? What tends to help you feel grounded again? How can you create more quiet space in your day, even when life is noisy?

* **"Why Is It So Hard to Simply Do Less?"** (p.117) questions the pressure to stay busy all the time. It invites us to consider whether doing less might actually lead to more peace, focus, and meaning. Why is slowing down sometimes the hardest thing to do? If you had to remove one thing from your weekly routine, what might that look like?

* **"What Success Might Look Like at Age ___"** (p.119) suggests that success changes depending on where you are in life—and that's okay. It encourages us to think about what truly matters, beyond money or applause. What does success mean to you right now, in this stage of your life? How has your view of success changed as you've grown?

REFLECTION QUESTIONS — BLURBS PT 3

❖ **"Stop Seeing Life as a Thing to Do"** (p.123) invites us to see life not as a to-do list, but as a gift of relationships and moments. It reminds us that loving our God, our family, our neighbors, and ourselves should take precedence over productivity. What's something you've done recently just for the joy of it—not because it was productive? How would your daily life change if your top priority was something other than productivity?

❖ **"The Dance"** (p.125) uses dancing as a metaphor for relationships—sometimes you lead, sometimes you follow, and sometimes you just need to listen for the rhythm of the song. Healthy connection takes practice, trust, and a willingness to give and take. What does it mean to be a good "dance partner" in your closest relationships? How do you know when to take the lead and when to follow someone else's lead with love and respect?

❖ **"Parenting a Child with a Disability"** (p.127) reflects on the unique joys and heartbreaks of raising a child with non-typical needs. It challenges us to slow down and see the world differently—through the lens of their uniqueness and as their strongest advocate. What does it mean to truly support and understand someone whose experience is different from your own? How has your life been touched in some way by a person living with a disability?

❖ **"The Five Love Destroyers"** (p.131) explores five common patterns that can harm relationships if left unchecked—things like blame, resentment, and withdrawal. It invites us to pay attention and take small steps toward healing. Which of these five love destroyers do you think is the easiest to fall into? Which one would be the most devastating to you?

❖ **"Some Things I've Learned About Grief"** (p.133) offers honest reflections on what grief feels like—messy, unpredictable, and deeply personal. It reminds us that grief doesn't follow a timeline, and it doesn't mean we're broken. Have you experienced grief in your life? If so, what has it looked like for you?

❖ **"In Defense of Settling"** (p.137) pushes back against the idea that we should always want more. It argues that sometimes, peace and contentment are better than endless striving. When have you found peace in "enough"? How do you know when it's time to chase a dream and when it's time to take rest in what you already have?

❖ **"The Infinite Within"** (p.141) suggests that each of us holds something vast and powerful inside—a connection to something bigger than ourselves. It challenges us to live with wonder and intention. What does it feel like to be connected to something greater than yourself? When in your life have you felt a type of connection to something beyond your understanding?

❖ **"Life Is a Moment"** (p.143) reminds us to fill the moment we live in with the things that matter most. What matters most to you? If you could give one piece of life advice to someone younger than you, what would it be?

www.ingramcontent.com/pod-product-compliance
Lightning Source LLC
Chambersburg PA
CBHW060647260626
47161CB00008B/3031

* 9 7 9 8 9 9 2 7 3 1 9 1 0 *